AF338291

"Somewhere, something incredible
is waiting to be known."

- Carl Sagan

The
Planets

WRITTEN & ILLUSTRATED BY
MICHAEL JAMIESON

FOR MY FAVOURITE STARGAZERS
HENRY & ISABELLA

Orbiting around
the Sun, so high,
are planets floating
above the sky.

Mercury is the
closest one,
the closest planet
to the Sun.

Spinning backwards
in outer space,
Venus is the
hottest place.

Earth, the home to
animals and trees,
is covered in land
and deep blue seas.

Many a spaceship has
launched towards Mars,
the bright red planet
amongst the stars.

Jupiter, the largest
planet in the Milky Way,
is icy and stormy
every day.

A gaseous giant
surrounded by rings,
Saturn has been admired
by ancient kings.

Uranus is an icy titan,
a planet the Sun can
barely brighten.

The very farthest
from the Sun,
Neptune is
the coldest one.

The Solar System

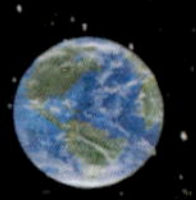

JUPITER

SATURN

URANUS
NEPTUNE

THE SUN

Average Surface Temperature: 5,500°C (9,932°F)
Average Internal Temperature: 15 million °C (27 million °F)
Diameter: 1,391,016 km (864,337 mi)
Starting from the centre of the Solar System, light from the Sun takes eight minutes to reach Earth.

MERCURY

Distance from the Sun: 57.9 million km (35.9 million mi)
Average Temperature: 167°C (333°F)
Diameter: 4,879 km (3,031 mi)
Length of Day: 59 days
Length of Year: 88 days
Mercury is the smallest planet in the Solar System.

VENUS

Distance from the Sun: 108.2 million km (67.2 million mi)
Average Temperature: 464°C (867.4°F)
Diameter: 12,104 km (7,521 mi)
Length of Day: 243 days
Length of Year: 225 days
After the Moon and the Sun, Venus is the brightest object in the Solar System.

EARTH

Distance from the Sun: 149.6 million km (92.9 million mi)
Average Temperature: 15°C (59°F)
Diameter: 12,756 km (7,926 mi)
Length of Day: 23 hours 56 minutes
Length of Year: 365 days 5 hours 48 minutes
Water covers 70% of the Earth's surface, and it is the only known planet to support life.

MARS

Distance from the Sun: 227.9 million km (141.6 million mi)
Average Temperature: -65°C (-85°F)
Diameter: 6,792 km (4,220 mi)
Length of Day: 24 hours 37 minutes
Length of Year: 687 days
Mars is nicknamed "The Red Planet" because of the layer of red dust on its surface.

JUPITER

Distance from the Sun: 778 million km (483.4 million mi)
Average Temperature: -110°C (-166°F)
Diameter: 142,984 km (88,846 mi)
Length of Day: 9 hours 55 minutes
Length of Year: 11 years 315 days
Jupiter is the largest planet in the Solar System.

SATURN

Distance from the Sun: 1,433 billion km (890 billion mi)
Average Temperature: -140°C (-220°F)
Diameter: 120,536 km (74,897 mi)
Length of Day: 10 hours 39 minutes
Length of Year: 29 years 163 days
Saturn, with its rings of ice and rock, has been observed since ancient times.

URANUS

Distance from the Sun: 2,872 billion km (1,784 billion mi)
Average Temperature: -195°C (-320°F)
Diameter: 5,118 km (3,223 mi)
Length of Day: 17 hours 14 minutes
Length of Year: 84 years 6 days
Uranus is the only planet that orbits the Sun on its side.

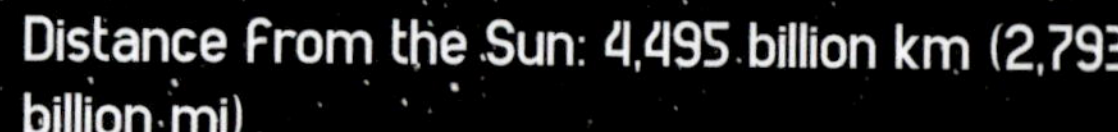

NEPTUNE

Distance from the Sun: 4,495 billion km (2,793 billion mi)
Average Temperature: -200°C (-330°F)
Diameter: 49,244 km (30,598 mi)
Length of Day: 16 hours 6 minutes
Length of Year: 164 years 288 days
The wind on Neptune can travel at 2,100 km per hour (1,304 mi per hour).